Date: 8/9/12

J 640 BOO
Boothroyd, Jennifer,
From washboards to
washing machines :

LIGHTNING
BOLT
BOOKS™

From Washboards to Washing Machines

How Homes Have Changed

Jennifer Boothroyd

Lerner Publications Company
Minneapolis

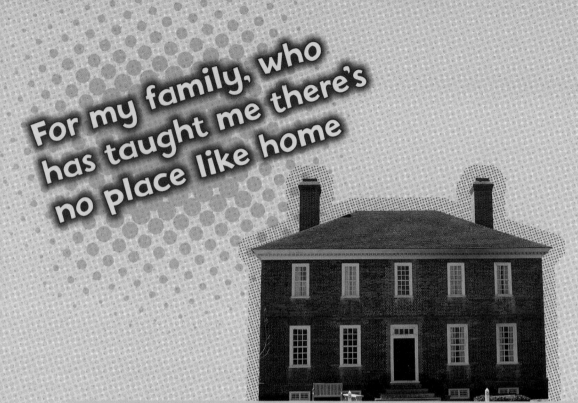

For my family, who has taught me there's no place like home

Lerner Publications Company
A division of Lerner Publishing Group, Inc.
241 First Avenue North
Minneapolis, MN 55401 U.S.A.

Website address: www.lernerbooks.com

Library of Congress Cataloging-in-Publication Data

Boothroyd, Jennifer, 1972–
    From washboards to washing machines: how homes have changed / by Jennifer Boothroyd.
       p. cm. — (Lightning bolt books™—Comparing past and present)
    Includes index.
    ISBN 978-0-7613-6747-5 (lib. bdg. : alk. paper)
    1. Household appliances—Juvenile literature. 2. Home economics—Juvenile literature. I. Title.
  TX298.B66 2012
    640—dc22   2010048831

Manufactured in the United States of America
1 — CG — 7/15/11

Contents

Home, Sweet Home

A home is a basic need.
Homes give people shelter and
a place to rest.

The homes we live in come in all shapes and sizes. Homes have changed over time.

Living in the Home

In the past, people heated rooms with radiators. Hot water flowed through pipes. The pipes warmed the air nearby.

Radiators were often noisy. They would hiss and clank.

These days, radiators still heat many homes. But people use furnaces to heat their homes too.

Furnaces can be set to change the temperature at different times.

In the past, people used
electric fans to keep cool
on hot days.

These days, many people still use electric fans. But air conditioners also help people beat the heat.

Air conditioners can cool a whole room or even a whole floor.

In the past, people usually got water from a faucet.

Water flows into homes through pipes.

These days, people still get water from faucets. But people can get water from some refrigerators too.

In the past, people lit their homes with incandescent lightbulbs. These bulbs make light by heating a wire inside the bulb.

Incandescent means "bright and glowing."

These days, many people use new types of lightbulbs. Fluorescent lights and LED lights last longer than the old bulbs. They use less power to make light.

This LED night-light is small but very bright.

Cleaning in the Home

People do lots of cleaning inside a home. In the past, people cleaned their laundry on washboards.

Washboards were tools with a bumpy surface. People rubbed their clothes against the surface to clean them.

These days, people use washing machines.

Washing machines make doing laundry easier.

In the past, people hung wet clothes outside to dry after washing them.

Wooden clips called clothespins hold these clothes up so they can dry.

These days, some people still hang their clothes up to dry. But they use clothes dryers too.

Dryers use heat and electricity to dry clothes.

In the past, people washed dirty dishes in the sink.

These days, many homes have a dishwasher. But some people still use their hands.

Dishwashers use less water than a person washing dishes by hand.

In the past, people pushed large, heavy vacuums across their carpets. The vacuums sucked up dirt.

These days, vacuums are much smaller. Some vacuums even move by themselves.

Cooking in the Home

People cook food in their kitchens. In the past, people used electric or gas stoves to heat food.

These days,
people cook food
in microwave
ovens too.

In the past, many homes had an icebox. These cabinets held big blocks of ice to keep food cold.

This man gets ready to deliver blocks of ice to use in iceboxes.

These days, most homes have refrigerators. Refrigerators use electricity to keep food cold.

Homes have gone through many changes.

Even so, our need for homes has not changed.

Names to Know

These people helped to improve other people's lives at home.

Thomas Alva Edison: Other inventors had created lightbulbs long before

Thomas Edison gave it a try. But Edison was the first to make a lightbulb stay lit for many hours at a time. He created his bulb in 1879.

Joseph C. Gayetty: In 1857, Joseph C. Gayetty invented packaged toilet paper. He called it Gayetty's Medicated Paper. A flat stack of five hundred sheets sold for 50 cents. Before 1857, people used old catalog pages or newspapers.

James Murray Spangler:
James Spangler invented
the suction sweeper in 1907.
He partnered with William
Hoover in 1908. Together,
they created the Hoover
Model O vacuum cleaner.
This 40-pound (18-kilogram) vacuum
cleaner ran on electricity.

Percy L. Spencer: Percy L. Spencer
invented the microwave oven. He built
the first microwave oven in 1947. It
weighed 750 pounds (340 kg)
and stood over 5 feet (1.5
meters) tall. Microwaves
became smaller and
more convenient. By
1994, more than 90
percent of American
homes had one.

Glossary

faucet: the part of the sink used to turn the water on and off

fluorescent: a type of lightbulb that sends out light from glowing gas

furnace: a machine that produces heat in a building

icebox: a place to keep food cold with large blocks of ice

incandescent: a type of lightbulb that sends out light from a glowing wire

LED: a small but bright lightbulb. *LED* stands for light-emitting diode.

microwave oven: an oven that uses microwaves to cook food

radiator: a machine that gives off heat from the flow of hot water inside it

washboard: a board with a bumpy surface that people used for washing clothes

Further Reading

EERE Kids: My Energy-Smart Home
http://www1.eere.energy.gov/kids/smart_home.html

Heinz, Brian. *Nathan of Yesteryear and Michael of Today*. Minneapolis: Millbrook Press, 2007.

Nelson, Robin. *Home Then and Now*. Minneapolis: Lerner Publications Company, 2003.

Rosenbaum, Stephanie. *Williams-Sonoma: Fun Food*. New York: Free Press, 2006.

Index

Photo Acknowledgments

The images in this book are used with the permission of: © Michael Joner/Dreamstime. com, p. 2; © Peter Vanderwarker/Riser/Getty Images, p. 4; © George Marks/Retrofile/ Getty Images, pp. 5 (top), 22; © Richard Majlinder/Dreamstime.com, p. 5 (bottom); © Bettmann/CORBIS, pp. 6, 29 (bottom); © Sebastian Czapnik/Dreamstime.com, p. 7; © Frank Scherchel/Time & Life Pictures/Getty Images, p. 8; © Bruce Laurance/Riser/ Photodisc/Getty Images, p. 9; © William Gottlieb/CORBIS, pp. 10, 26 (top); © iStockphoto.com/Kyoungil Jeon, p. 11; © James Warren/Dreamstime.com, p. 12; © iStockphoto.com/Alan Aga, p. 13; © Sasha/Hulton Archive/Getty Images, p. 14; © i love images/Alamy, p. 15; © H. Armstrong Roberts/Retrofile/Getty Images, p. 16; © Yellow Dog Productions/Lifesize/Getty Images, p. 17; © Harold M. Lambert/Archive Photos/Getty Images, p. 18; © Monkey Business Images/Dreamstime.com, p. 19; © H. Armstrong Roberts/ClassicStock/The Image Works, p. 20; © Douglas McFadd/Getty Images, p. 21; © Jupiterimages/FoodPix/Getty Images, p. 23; © Underwood & Underwood/CORBIS, p. 24; © Apple Tree House/Taxi/Getty Images, p. 25; © Universal Images Group/Collection Mix: Subjects/Getty Images, p. 26 (bottom); © Ariel Skelley/ Blend Images/Getty Images, p. 27; Library of Congress, p. 28 (LC-USZ62-105139); Courtesy of Hoover Historical Center/Walsh University, North Canton, Ohio, p. 29 (top); © Fotografkinja/Dreamstime.com, p. 30; © Fotosearch/Archive Photos/Getty Images, p. 31.

Front cover: © George Marks/Retrofile/Getty Images (top); © Flying Colours Ltd/Digital Vision/Getty Images (bottom).

Main body text set in Johann Light 30/36.